Prepper Penguin
and
The Goal Monster

CATHRYN PERRY. CATHY GRUSS. KICHAN SVETLANA

DEDICATION by CATHY GRUSS
Founder of Vision Partying

I dedicate this book to my loving mama and papa, who have inspired and supported me to become the creative, entrepreneurial, independent woman that I am today. Also, to my loving and dedicated husband, who has encouraged me to soar beyond all that I ever thought I could. And to my beautiful children, who have always motivated me to learn and grow.

Max, Addison, and Violet walked home from school, enjoying a snack, "Did you see that game last night?" Max asked his friends.

"I was too busy watching my new favorite artist on my laptop. He is a guitar player who sings, and he's amazingly gifted," Addison replied.

Violet just stared down at the paper in her hand, "I was playing video games, but maybe I should have been studying for the spelling test," she sighed.

The friends stopped and laid in the grass in Violet's front yard.

"How do I get to be as good as that player? I'm good at sports, but I want to be, like, professional," Max remarked.

"I just want to be better at spelling. I just don't get it. It is so frustrating!" Violet added.

"I wish I could play guitar like a real musician, I wasn't born with that kind of gift, though," Addison confessed.

All three kids let out a big SIGH. "I practice, but I don't see myself getting better. I'll never be a professional athlete," Max said.

"I don't even know how to start," Addison cried. "I'll never get that good!"

"Guys, maybe some people just have "it," and some don't. It's seriously just a mystery," replied Violet.

"Oh, you guys! It's no mystery! You just need the right tools!"

"Whoa!" All three friends were shocked to see a penguin on the lawn,

"Who are you!?" they yelped.

"I'm Prepper Penguin! With my toolbox of friends, I look for kids just like you who need help to reach their goals. All your goals are possible as long as you plan, prepare, and take action!" smiled the little penguin.

"But, being an athlete, a musician, a top student—those are all very different goals. Monster-sized goals," Addison commented.

"You are right," Prepper cheered. "But, all goals can be reached by following the same steps!"

"Big and scary like a monster too. Besides, if we don't have the talent to be that good, we will never get there," Max replied.

Prepper leaned in, "You know, there is a saying out there that luck is just hard work in disguise! All the things you guys want to get better at are skills, and improving your skills takes practice and focus. People aren't just talented, lucky, and gifted to get to be the best at what they want to do, they choose to work for it — every day. You can too! My friends and I would be happy to show you how. Ready to learn?"

"I'm in!" Max agreed.

"Me, too!" Addison smiled.

"Me, three!" Violet squealed.

"Alright crew, you heard them! Time to show these kids how to make their vision a reality!" Prepper set his toolbox down.

It started to shake, twirl, and bounce!

Out flew a paintbrush, scissors, and glue!
Out jumped a pen, a notepad, and stickers too!

"Woohoo!" Brush yelled.

"Let's get started!" Glue hollered.

"First, I want to show these kids how to get started at home. I'll need you all to start a special project for us in the meantime. We need a big goal puzzle. A monster goal puzzle!"

"Come, show me your house, Violet. Together, we can figure out how to set the stage for your success! Max and Addison can watch and do the same things at their homes." Prepper waddled towards the door.

The tool kit got to work. Soon, snippets of paper were flying through the air.

Violet swung open her bedroom door, "Taa-Daa!"

Prepper, Addison and Max gasped, "Oh. My."

"Here's an idea. Let's clean off this desk and put the dirty clothes in the basket. It is easier to study when we have a clean space to work."

To-do List!!
☑ study at 7PM - 9PM
☑ practicing spelling for 10 min
☐ read a book

"Now, let's put up a notepad to make a schedule of reminders. When we write down our goals, they become more real and easier to go for. So, every morning, write down three goals you have for the day. One could be practicing spelling for ten minutes.

For Addison, it could be to watch a guitar tutorial or practice a chord. For Max, it could be to do 10 pushups and squats to get stronger! The second and third goals could be to help the family with household chores, eat something healthy, or do something fun or relaxing.

When our three daily goals are balanced, our life is balanced. If you try to only work on one thing throughout the day, you will get burned out quickly. It is important to remember that big goals are a marathon and not a race. Lots of successful days add up to a successful life."

"Finally, let's set a timer on the desk with 10 minutes to start. When we have a timer counting down, we can focus and it lets us know it's not going to last forever. I know that practice, a studying session, a chore can feel like forever without a timer! When we know and see it's only for a set amount of time, it automatically feels easier!"

Looking around at her clean space and short list, Violet smiled. "I already feel better! I can do this!"

Outside, the tools had finished up the goal monster.

"We made one for each of you!" Scissors cheered.

"Use me to write your big goal on the monster side. Addison, your goal could be to play 2 songs on the guitar. Now, cut and glue pictures of your favorite guitar player, cool music you like, or draw yourself rocking out!" Paintbrush instructed.

Prepper penguin chimed in, "Then flip it over and on each of the puzzle pieces, write one thing you can do in one day to get better, like practice for ten minutes or watch a tutorial."

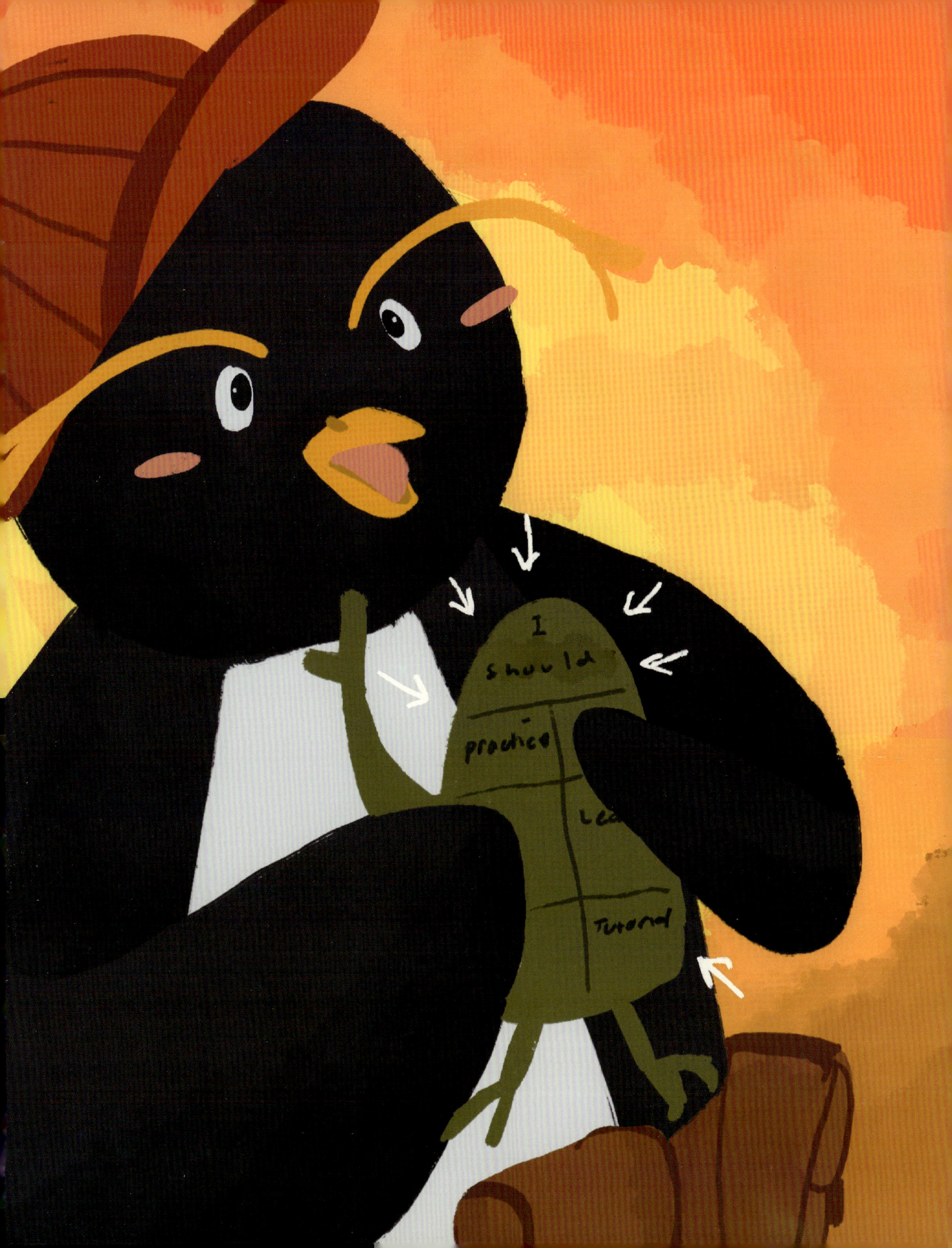
I
should
practice
Tutorial

Max glued his favorite sports stars on one side.
On the other, he wrote out different exercises
he could practice and books he could read to
grow his abilities.

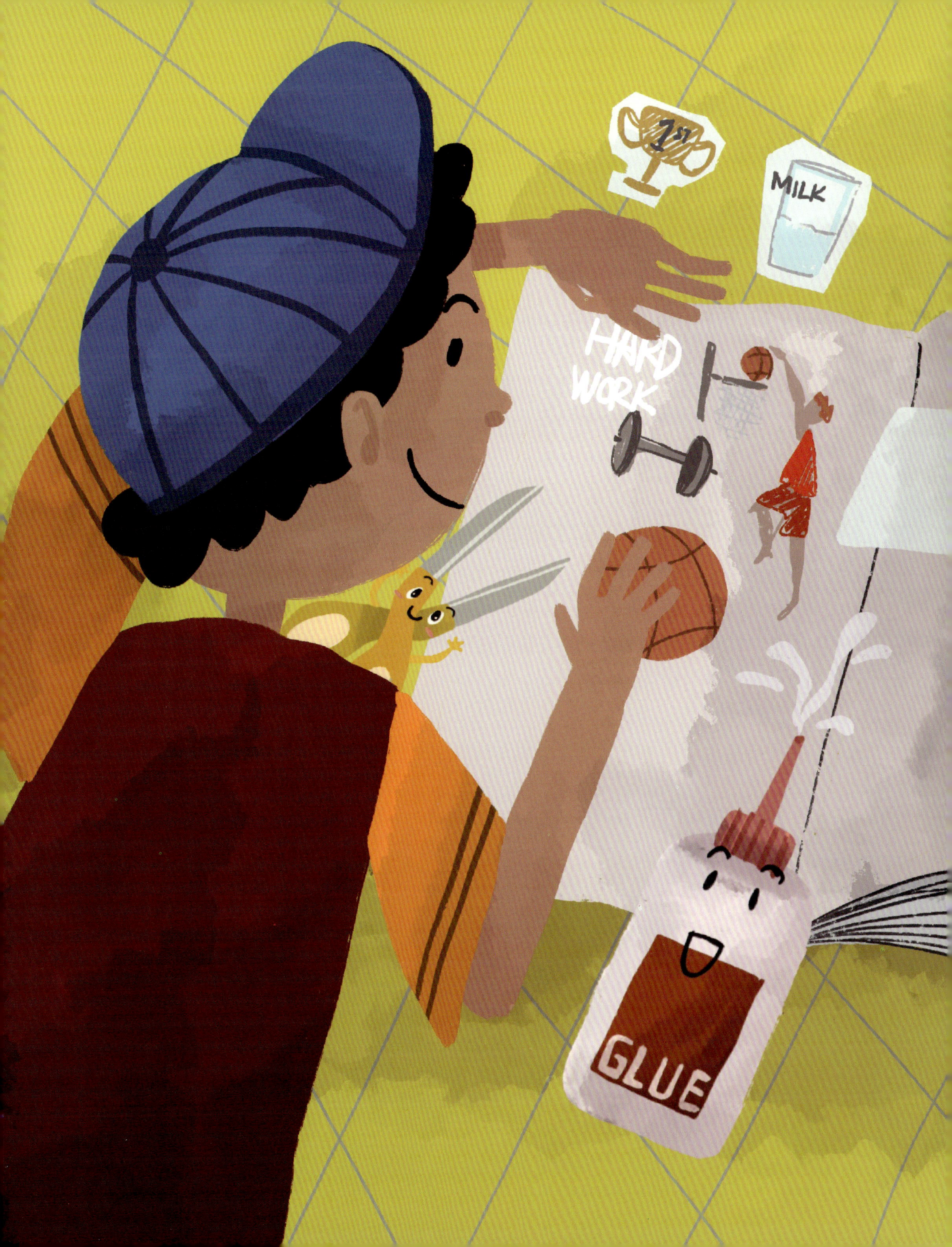
1st
MILK
HARD WORK
GLUE

Violet glued pictures of books and A+'s, along with successful women she looked up to. On the other side she wrote out books to read, ways to practice, and study ideas to help her improve her grades at school.

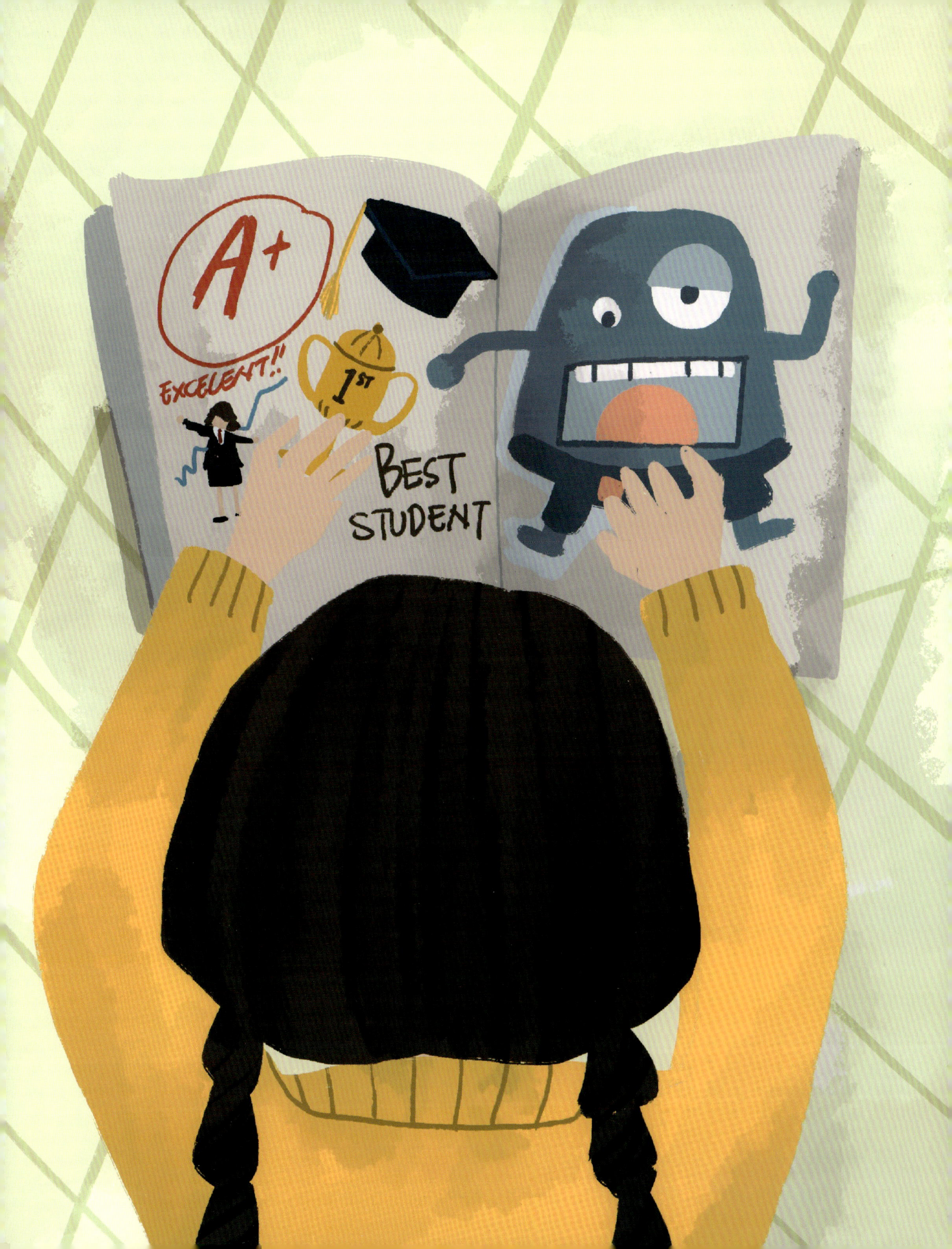
A+
EXCELENT!!
1ST
BEST STUDENT

"Time to cut!" Scissors yelled.

Prepper began, "Yep! Cut that big monster goal into pieces! Take one pocket-sized piece with you each day to remind yourself to work on that piece of the goal. Each time you complete one, you can tape it together to rebuild your monster goal and see how you've grown!"

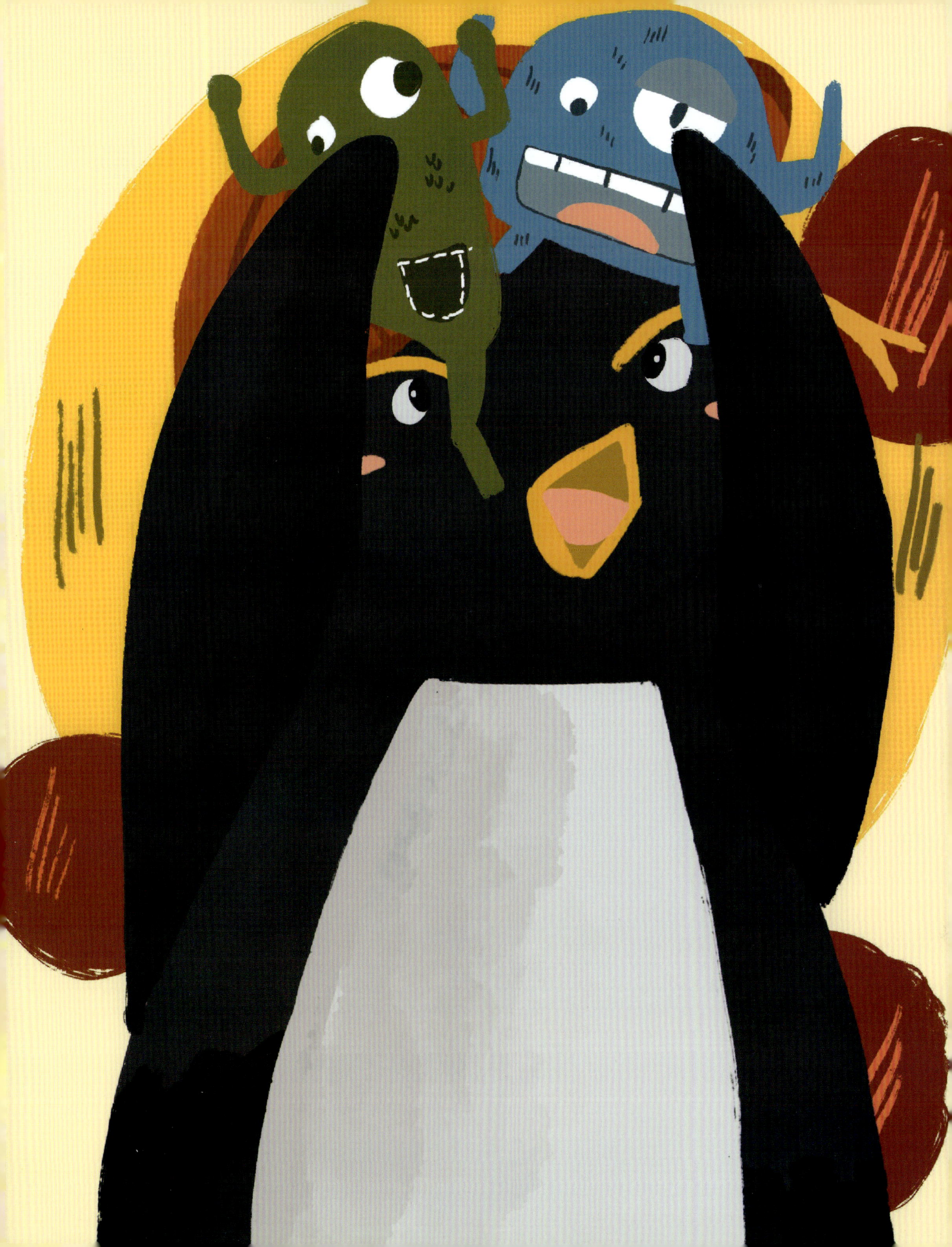

Are **YOU** ready to breakdown your monster goals?

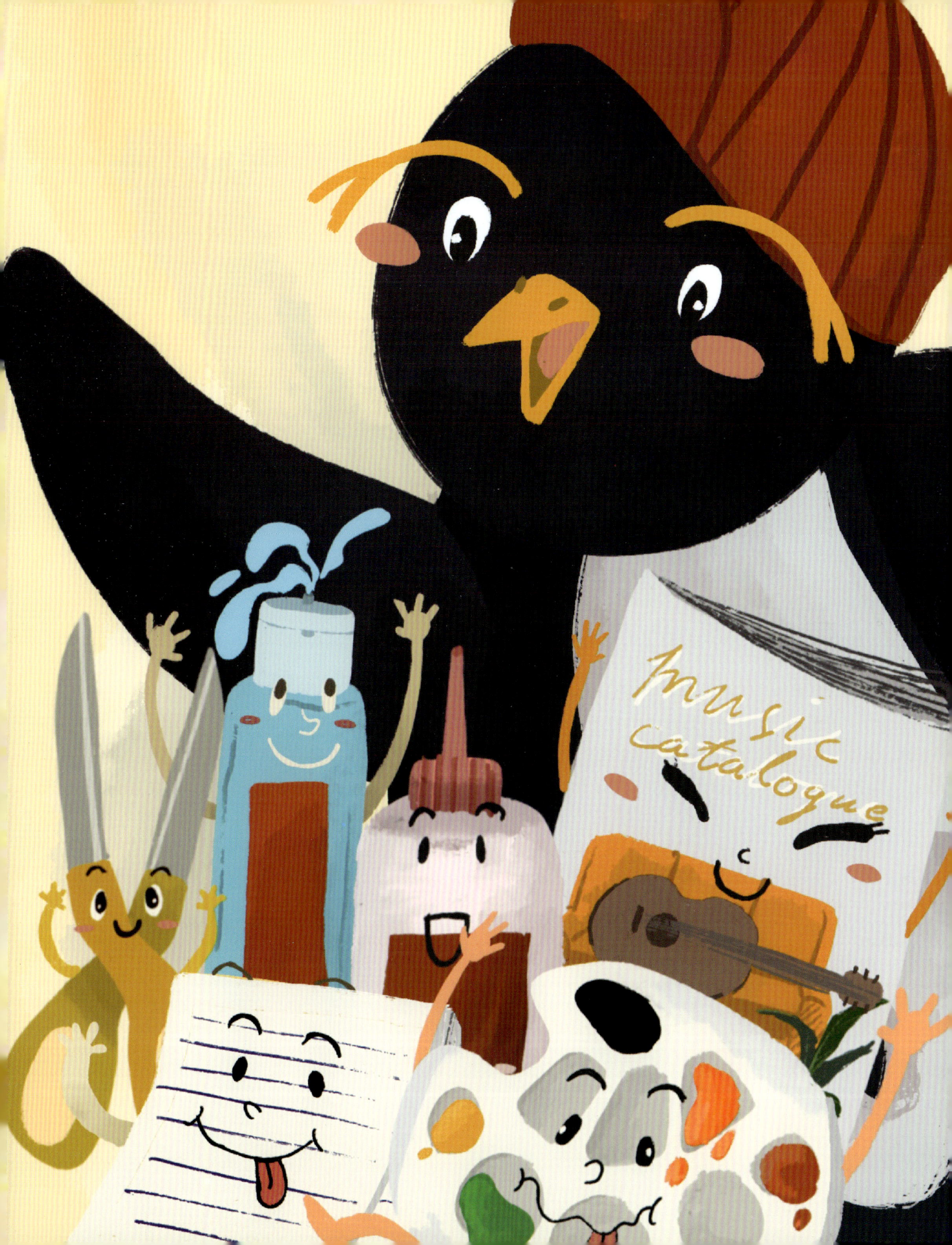
music
catalogue

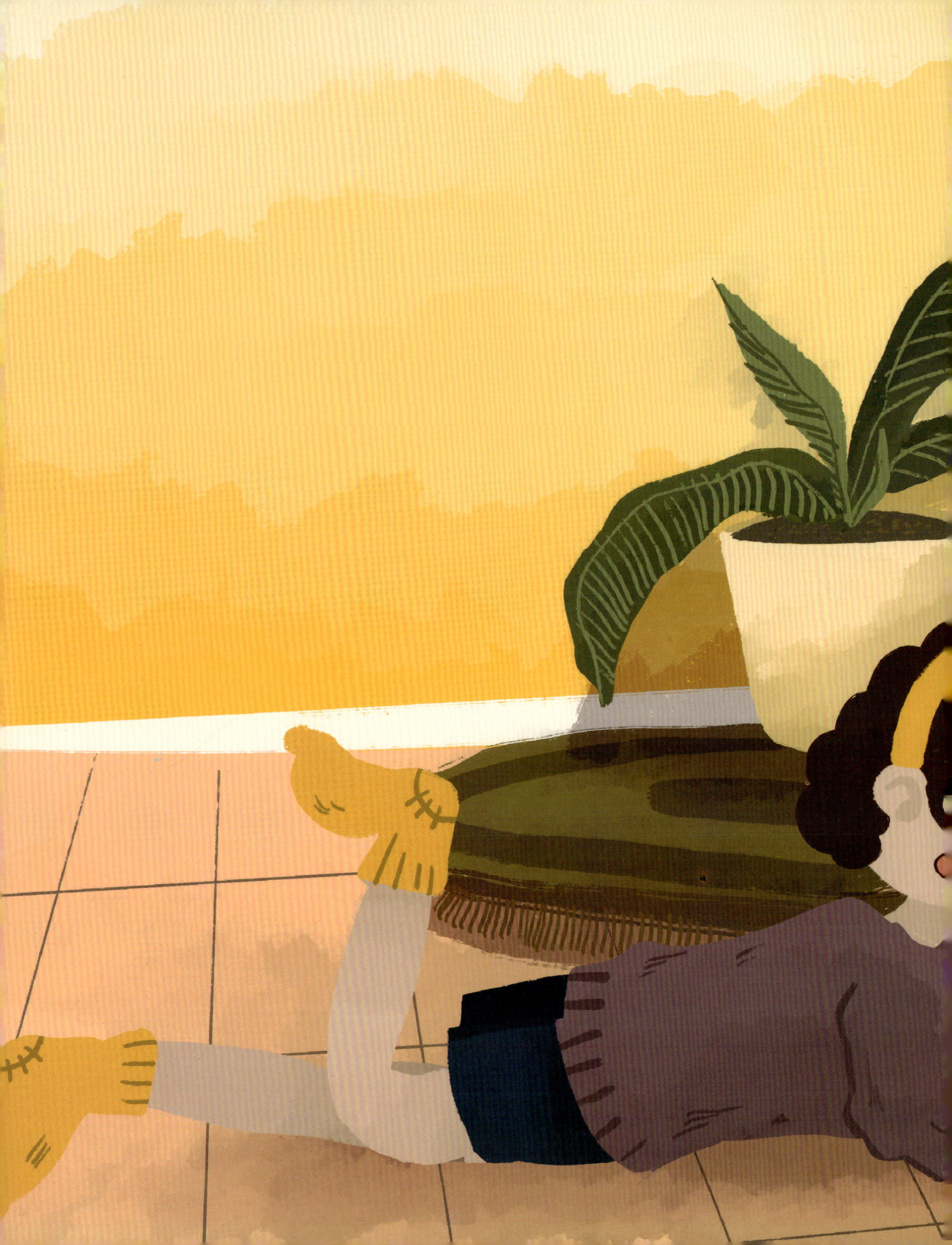

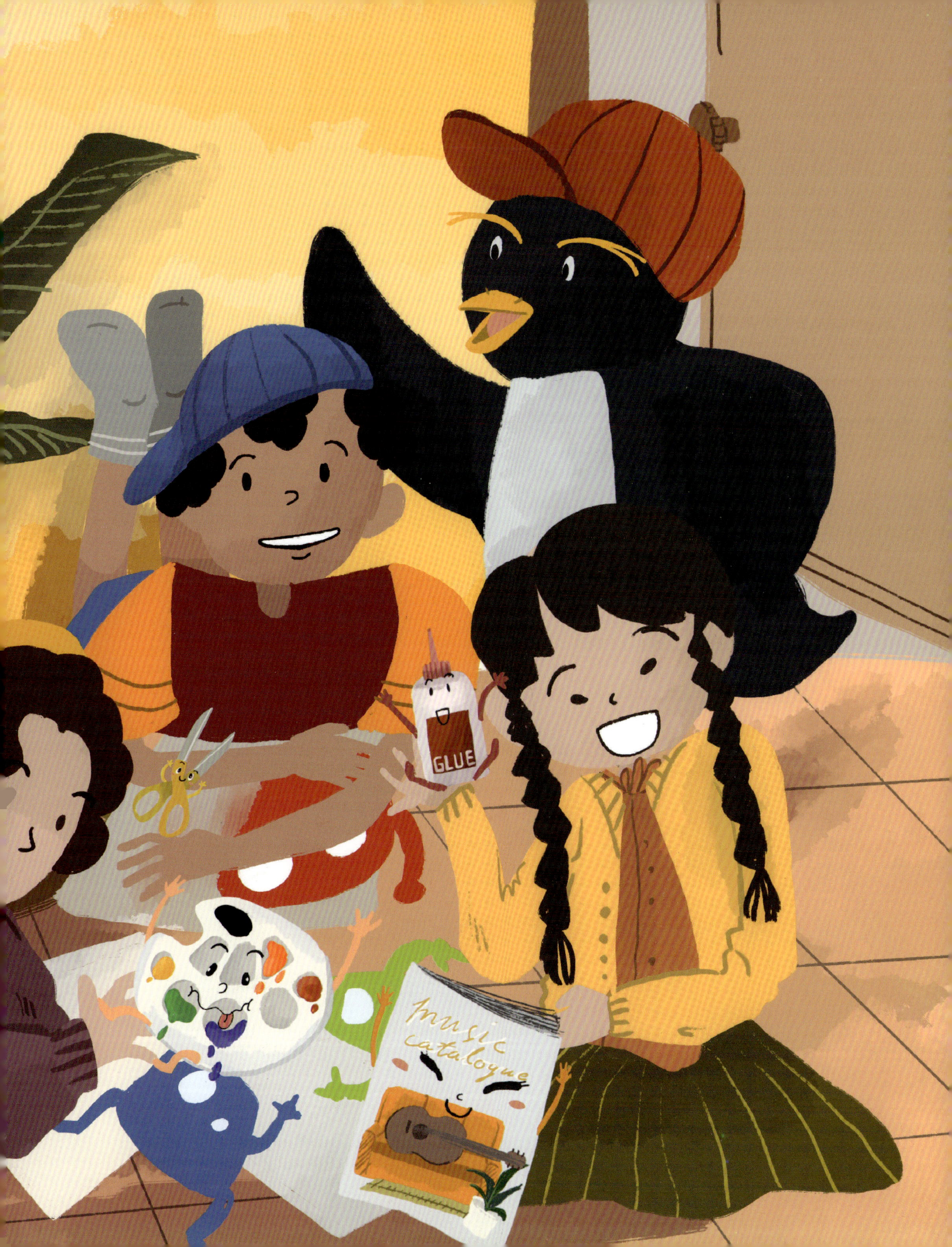
GLUE
music catalogue

ACTIVITY SHEETS

For more fun, check out our website at VisionPartying.com!

WHAT ARE MY GOALS?

Time to Brainstorm!
Brainstorming can help you decide what your goals are, and even which one you want to focus on. Take a moment to think about what makes you excited. What are you passionate about? Think of something that you love to learn about or do.

I like to …

I like to …

I am good at …

I am good at …

I love …

I feel happy when …

I want to be …

illustration by kichan

MY GOALS

Hi! My name is Addison.
I love listening to music and watching my favorite band Perfom.
When I hear my song play, I feel happy and excited.
My goal is to learn to play guitar.

What do you want to do? What is your goal?
Write it here.

_____

> Goals can be BIG
> Goals can be small
> When we have the right vision
> We can accomplish them ALL !!

My Big Goals

_____
_____
_____
_____
_____

My Small Goals

_____
_____
_____
_____
_____

MOST IMPORTANT NOW (MIN)

When you are ready to work towards your goal, whether it is big or small it is important to figure out where to start! A simple trick that leads to success is to write down all the actions you can take to help you reach your goal. Oh No! There are so many! Let's figure out how to pick your MIN action. That is that action that you decide is most important now.

Here is Addison. She wants to learn to play guitar. Addison has several good ideas on what she can do to help her get better.

- Watch music videos
- Watch a guitar tutorial and follow along
- Read a book about guitars
- Learn about reading musical notes
- Listen to her favorite band
- Take a guitar lesson

Some good ideas, right? But which one is the MOST IMPORTANT NOW? What is the best action Addison can take first to learn to play guitar? What action do you think is least important?

Your turn! Draw yourself in the square. We are going to work on your goal now. Write down your ideas on what action you could take to work towards that goal? Circle the one you think is MIN.

illustration by Vichan

MONSTER GOAL REFLECTION

What is your monster goal?

How can a monster goal puzzle help you to reach your goals?

Taking small steps everyday can help you accomopolish your BIG goals

TRUE or FALSE

Brainstorming can help you find your goals

TRUE or FALSE

What does MIN stand for?

What tools do you need to make a monster goal puzzle?

Who is your favorite character from The Prepper Penguin story?

"You can do anything if you set goals. You just have to push yourself." —RJ Mitte

illustration by kichan

MY JOURNAL PAGE

I am grateful for _____

_____

I am happy about _____

_____

One thing I would change about today is _____

_____

One way I can avoid distactions is _____

_____

A challenge I had this week was _____

_____

If I could do one thing all day, I would _____

_____

TIME TOWARDS MY GOAL RECORDING SHEET

What I did to work towards my goal	Minutes spent

"There are only two rules for being successful. One, figure out exactly what you want to do, and two, do it." — Mario Cuomo

For more fun
Check out our website at VisionPartying.com!